T0160714

BOOKS BY CATHERINE WAGNER

My New Job (Fence Books, 2009)

Macular Hole (Fence Books, 2004)

Miss America (Fence Books, 2001)

NERVOUS DEVICE

CITY LIGHTS SPOTLIGHT SERIES NO. 8

CATHERINE WAGNER

NERVOUS

DEVICE

CITY LIGHTS

SAN FRANCISCO

CITY LIGHTS SPOTLIGHT
The City Lights Spotlight Series was founded in 2009, and is
edited by Garrett Caples.

Library of Congress Cataloging-in-Publication Data
Wagner, Catherine.
Nervous device / Catherine Wagner.
p. cm. — (City Lights spotlight series ; no. 8)
Poems.
ISBN 978-0-87286-565-5
I. Title.
PS3573.A3693N47 2012
811'.54—dc22
2012025575

The editor would like to thank Rebecca Wolff of Fence, Jasmine Moorhead
and Kendy Genovese of the Weinstein Gallery, and Richard Overstreet
for the Leonor Fini Estate for their generous assistance with this book.

Cover Image: Leonor Fini. *Femme costumée (Femme en armure)* [detail] ©
1938. Oil on canvas, 13 ¾ x 9 ½ inches. © Estate of Leonor Fini, courtesy
Weinstein Gallery. Photo: Nicholas Pishvanov.

All City Lights Books are distributed to the trade by
Consortium Book Sales and Distribution: www.cbsd.com

For small press poetry titles by this author and others,
visit Small Press Distribution: www.spdbooks.com

City Lights Books are published at the City Lights Bookstore,
261 Columbus Avenue, San Francisco, CA 94133
www.citylights.com

CONTENTS

NOTES AND ACKNOWLEDGMENTS

This book's working title, "The Bounding Line," quoted the catalog essay for William Blake's only exhibition, a failure staged above his brother's hosiery shop in Golden Square. In the essay, Blake defends the importance of the bounding line for differentiating figures. When Jem Sportsman interviewed me about audience and what is the bounding line, at some point I discussed my tilted cervix and said that "if you"—if she—"put in" his "finger just a few inches" she would "feel it—here—" and then I stuck out my fist and had him put her figure inside it which freaked him out though not as much as if I'd offered her my vagina to put his finger in. Later in the interview we referred back to that moment—when I wanted (and she went along) to imply to the audience that we was putting his finger in my vagina and touching my cervix—we said "for the sake of the interview of course" "yes of course, for the sake of the interview, heh heh," to imply boundary.

"A Well Is a Mine : A Good Belongs to Me" adapts lines from the sea shanty "Where Am I to Go Me Johnnies." "Capitulation to the Total Poem" collages Alice Notley's *Culture of One* and Aaron Kunin's PMLA essay "Shakespeare's Preservation Fantasy." It is printed on the outside of a bangle meant to be put on and taken off while the poem is read. The title of "The Autonomy of Art Has Its Origins in the Concealment of Labor" is from Adorno as quoted in Ramor Ryan's translation of Raúl Zibechi's *Dispersing Powers: Social Movements as Anti-State Forces*. "A Landscape" quotes John Milton's Nativity Ode. "Do Fairly Pleasant Thing" riffs on Robert Duncan's poem "Often I Am Permitted to Return to a Meadow." I am grateful to the Canadian filmmaker Katherine Knight for soliciting writing on color for a film on the Canadian painter Wanda Koop; the series "INFRA RES: Color Essays" resulted, though the poems were not used, as far as I know. They are influenced by (and occasionally quote) Josef Albers' *Interaction of Color* and Michel-Eugène Chevreul's *The Principles of Harmony and Contrast of Colors*. A Wallace Foundation fellowship funded a summer residency at Millay Colony during which part of this book was written; my thanks to the Foundation and to the Millay staff. Versions of these poems appeared in *Abraham Lincoln, Archive of the Now, The Awl, Brooklyn Rail, Cambridge Literary Review, Catch Up, Claudius App, Colorado Review, Double Room, Fence, Flying Object, Lana Turner, The Millay Colony Newsletter, Morpheme, New American Writing, On and On Screen, Painted, Spoken, Pinwheel, Poem-A-Day* (Academy of American Poets website), *Poetry Time Anthology, Poor Claudia, Rampike, Smoking Glue Gun*, and the Dusi/e 2010 Chapbook Series.

Gratitude to all the editors. Thanks to Jody Bates, cris cheek, Martin Corless-Smith, Linda Russo, Keith Tuma, Dana Ward, and Rebecca Wolff for comments on versions of the manuscript, and to Garrett Caples at City Lights for all his work and help. And to friends and family, especially Ambrose.

•

Catherine Wagner publishes with Fence Books. Founded in 1998 by Rebecca Wolff, *Fence* is a biannual journal of poetry, fiction, art, and criticism that has a mission to redefine the terms of accessibility by publishing challenging writing distinguished by idiosyncrasy and intelligence rather than by allegiance with camps, schools, or cliques. Launched in 2001, Fence Books publishes poetry, fiction, and critical texts and anthologies, and prioritizes sustained support for its authors.

NERVOUS DEVICE

PRESSED GO

I was ruling the world with you, which is, everyone's decision about anything was valve to next.

Continuez, in the time-braid incorp:

dust of continent, yeast infection, mercury glint invisibly wet, increasingly limited bestiary song, view from mountains I must drive to, apartments flare their parking lot huge cracked black skirts. Fat mud thighs process runoff.

Dear Garrett (editor),

Funny to be moved by exigencies of market to write poems, to deadline, out of time "must write poems to fill the huge demand for them."

Poem as blister formed through friction, swelled atoll, sucked fluid from the body of the host. I made no money from my poems but they statused me.

Instead of tearing down the poem (scrape it D&C and exit), I made more shapely baubs, that pleasure me, hum crystal when touched. All readers: take a union breath, trust me? for I started to know-what-I-was-doing in a poem, the intuition track laid out prior, poem aligns and rolls (if rickety) headlit and through the forest. When it instead should unalign and disembark the trees.

G, you wanted poems and I trapped them in a book, guinea foul their cage, doggerel blockprint gridlock fossil.

Pixels screen what powers screens: waterfalls and turbines. Falls disappear granular down turbine funnel. But the eye need not follow any each droplet. Can watch falls quiver white static. Screen for use.

Articulate the choice between action and understanding. The poem to order. Write it cause. Thighs klutz beneath my skirt.

Dear art surface.

A WELL IS A MINE : A GOOD BELONGS TO ME

Wide-winged heaven
  mowed my garden down:
blacklily puddle.   Let commerce
suck brights from all dally-halls
 and string them christmas mines.

Will folded, made a napkin
Old agendas used to clean my mouth
 of will.
I built this tone
 ironically; that is,
it goes against itself.

"Who is responsible for the oil spill in the Gulf?"
"Did you drive here?"

"I had no choice."
"Who took your choice?"

"If we don't have oil we'll need slaves, or none of us will ever read
    or paint."
"I don't see what's wrong with not getting paid, if you're getting

Fed and housed. I didn't get to choose whether I drove here.
I'll be a slave if it will save the planet."

"OK you're a slave."
"Textbook will say: 'Slavery became both colorblind and trendy.

Whether this was coincidence is matter for...'"
"But only 'one in ten men is colorblind.' The rest of us

Might use color to decide who slaves will be."
"*De jure*, white contains all colors."

"*De jure*, it won't be that noticeable if we don't start with white
    people?"
"Anybody here who's *de facto* 'black'?"

[silence]

"I'm afraid to speak for anybody in a different identity category."
"And how many slaves will you need to maintain your standard of
         living sans oil?"

"A slave for the bicycle jitney. A lawnmowing slave.
A slave to cook and load compressed wood pellets into the wood
         stove.

I can do that. But then will need a slave to weed and clean."
"Three slaves per household?"

"Three to five."
"Will you be one of mine?"

"Let's all take turns!"
"Can't come to your birthday party, it's my slave week."

"Need categories of us."
"A use for identity politics."

"A use for identity. They also serve who only stand and wait."
"Heidegger called them 'standing reserve.'"

"If some of us are to be slaves, it's a good thing there's this income
   disparity."
"It does make it easier."

"A feudal system, stabilized—"
"By international trade."

"But freedom is a value."
"Say '*has* a value' and it can be traded."

"Freedom x Need = Reality."

"Freedom

$$\frac{\text{Freedom}}{\text{Reality}} = \text{Art.}$$

"Then Art x Reality = Freedom."

"Freedom

$$\frac{\text{Freedom}}{\text{Art}} = \text{Reality?}$$

"Where art is politics."

"*Where am I to go? Oh hey, hey, hey, Johnny, where am I to go?*"
"I *am where to go! I am where to go, dear Johnny.*"

"*What are you to me?*" "*Hey, hey, hey, Johnny—I'll tell you when
    you're mine.*"
"*Go our separate way together, tell me when you're mine.*"

COME HERE

FOR A

If
You're not against me
You're not with me
I do not need to say
I beg your pardon

Springy hairs on your chest
Who would you be against?
You would be with me
If you were against me
Trouble-maker.

I beg your pardon.

Unkempt pattern
Springy hairs on chest
Please to be against everyone
Nips like grommets.

RAIN COG

Think about cold genial.

Someone whose symbolic
Presence makes the
Liquid flush from pores in
My vaginal skin.   There.

And it works reversely—
Surge, seek source.

A nervous device, a communicator
The juice waits stupidly

Not shiny, because my pants are on.
The juice in shadow.

UNCLANG

I would like never to be obscure. I understand why I was: explaining
is a bore, and flattens lang, so, it takes experience to write a real poem
that is well-lit. Which is not the same as clear
drinking water from a jar, old
babydoll in bed. Broke and well-fed.

Lying here is great, I said,
you are not, nowhere, stay yup alnight.
You sunshine bleat.

I coulda moved to _____ moved to _____. My more glamor-
ous avatar did, she willy did, but when she was there, lookout, she
looked in her pocketbook at the mirror
in the snapshut clamshell, the mirror was distwatted
curved along the shell wall. A weirdo pronunciation from New
    Ywok,
distwatted. That's just dis toy bin and it's more exciting than the
fucking infernet.

Writing a poem is like reaching two prosthetic limbs out as far as you

can on either side to grab something in front of you. You can't grab
it but maybe you'll *take flight*.

But I'm not trying to grab anything in front of me when I write a
poem. GET that kitty.

INNOCENT MONEY

I must maintain
  our separation, boys
so that you will continue
to invest.
I like this stage,
   and would like to
   extend it.

Your lover is beyond
the proscenium arch
(you are audience
  and play in your own play).
She is/I am handling
my carcass
with strings.
We seek admiration.
At some point
  early in the playing

I enter my carcass
   to embrace you
—Our proscenium
foreheads touch
and I am shot with fear
 of boredom.
Actually you are
 controlling my carcass.

A PATTERN

Birdsong made the sun come up
and I will love you with this poem.

You take your turn as other.

If you understand
away and home, the pleasure of refrain,
let me make you feel as if meaning.

In my head, beloved.

CAPITULATION TO THE TOTAL POEM

Poem to be worn as a bracelet

If you put the [hand] inside, she will pop out: the imp to preserve culture wriggles under the worn. A part capable of dying capitulates to total enclosure in poem. Remove her (poem) from test subjects! Discard intercourse. O hovering over the desert, at midnight—poem removed from victims, extrapersonal.

PLEASURE TRIP

FOR JC-S

The reading just OK but I made friends with my friends.
Minivan moving, sun exit   gold blisses ground.

Fuzz-static branches overlap. Uncrumple, move past 'em,
 slay worry.

Last night bar-restaurant with Mel humor reactor gorgeous glinty
person, Rod hale alt-dude, Dan serious and explaining, cris across
from me laughing with Keith. Golden glory. I drank an appley cham-
pagne drink. Ate a pupusa. Had not embarrassed myself.

Razorcut bank of trees
ceases gray, goes stiff sharp black
like, like...is pattern, I like

don't want to get dark, this is the best sun. Lo,

what swanky love I got

ADULT STORE

ADULT VIDEO

I see like a grownup
adulterated sugar in my veins.
Type till it is all the way dark.

Alice back seat can see my screen. Make the point small.

Marvin Gaye drags me back to road trip, McCall, ID with Martin,
radio songs I explicated for him in unknowing telepathic access to his
sexual healing, a Beatles song I couldn't stand, the pain, if I, were to
tell you that our love, was in vain. So I dope. You'll see that I will love.

S. saying "He is so stupid" last night—reaction I often get from
friends—years later now—fearing partner's infection by broken
marriage. "He's a shit, he's such an idiot." Currency dropped in a
solidarity machine. I won't sleep with your husband but I am not in
that machine any more.

Martin told me when I gave him *Hole in the Ground* he read it in the airport hotel bar. The bartender asked what he was reading. He said "Poems by my ex-wife about how great her sex life is now." They're not about that. The bartender bought him a drink.

La Mer shop at Heathrow, Brosie two years old fascinated by the aquarium. He's fine, woman said, he's occupied, do you want a facial?/I can't afford anything here./That's OK, I'm not busy. Gentle pressure near tearducts—eyes shut, spilt: Am leaving him./ Oh honey. Here is a little jar. I don't usually give these for free. Put it on when you get on the plane. Your skin will be like butter when you land. Like cream.
I was tired and it was
Like aery silk. A silk bag for my sick. He got a drink and I got cream, for

free, the sentimental music is sending me. Puff of cloud from the power plant. Screen light off, type into dark. Sun almost dived. Aiming for it miles. Chasing it, will beat us.

The gold light blown off the grass. Soft green ellow fade. Every noon in my body is naked and loved. Can't remember what it was I came way fun. Not even here to memorize the crowd. Against my will I know looks like I move it but I'm sitting still. It's not cause I care it's gettin getting there.

This is the second part of my life and this poem
Where I will say though I won't listen
DON'T make anything crap. Abuse waste.

For Jeanne won't be slimming nay more. Jeanne of Jeanne light.
Tumor against her spine, growing. Airplane skinny against pearl
cloud inaudible, bomber, where's the base. Jeanne loved her sons
post-moral.

Jeanne is joan warrior. Shopping warrior. Generous, in material
love, love is made of stuff. I'll show you, I'll give it to you in a bag.
Come and look at it, I laid it out on the bed.

The puffy face, alcohol. Always peasant and charming.

The hermit crab leaves its shell to die. Spiral of sunsets, wake, sleep,
eat, shit; a brief focus, a fizzgold drink, best dancer at the wedding,
age 60. The young men wanted to dance with her. She said "Dance
with your husband!" / "He doesn't want to dance with me."

The dead my exlaw. Be binary like day night. Then you know where
you are. Alive dead. The time of you casts backwards. Time-swathe
is hers, bound in a roll.

Contain the growth in an eggshell light. Cannery piss.

Swells her body, crazing the cells, abundant cancer life. We put a
value on growth.

Look around at Alice, she smiles at me.

Then the sun says bye.
Frightens me, won't be able to see anything.
The driver will.
Going to be the driver, by the time we get to Columbus. Be careful
with the lives, minivanguard, Alice, Jonny, Keith, cris, Alla and me.

Trees finished being sharp. Twig froth
 into hypnosis, eyes squinch then the lips curl upward, furthermotor,
lips slacken and part, eyes slacken, too
shut to see whether it's dark. Sealed listening

colors near grayed out I slit in cloud place
find lout slant cloud pinkish cool of the evening mind, girls in
 summer clothes.
Stay with the young girls and the old, the strong women my age can
do anything already done.

Jeanne worked at a bar, at a shop, cleaned houses and hotels. Worked as a bookkeeper. Tough nude pantyhose, gold pumps, tweed blazer, goldish beige silk sweater underneath. Gold glasses. Golden hair dyed near white. Let it white.

She grew up in the blitz. House destroyed by bomb. Go home, house gone. It scared me so I never got over it, in my life. Said the lady. She sing most soberly. I asked her was she merry, she would not consent to be. You are the one I've chosen to be my dearest dear. Your cold hearth's frozen in you, locked up with all my fear, Light advancing The night is quite advancing it's near the break of day. Kind miss what do you say.

NEVER MIND

The terms given you were: Breathe. That starts it.
Then, do as you're told, to please them
  and don't, to discover your mind.
Then you are imperfect
  child, a wanton.
Whence came this agon? Snot and tears,
  hot face, and wretched powerless,
   except to cause annoy. So cause annoy.

VERSUS

In this poem all artifice
is stripped away
but you are held under water.

In this poem you enter a mirrored dressing room
lit so that you look more beautiful than you have ever looked.

I recognize you with surprise.
In this poem you are by yourself.

RAIN COG

One who could not smell came up to the other's apartment (threw pebbles at the window) after the other had masturbated. The other not having washed her hands brought one a beer. One was intimate with the other's smell and wanted to be intimate with the other and was and did not know it. *That* old factory.

RECENT MALE INTERVENTION

pressed on my, soft rhizome, ridgy whatfor, sense-data makes me
want to fuck more, have babies while still can. Why then did it hurt
when I was younger? Because it doesn't matter if you like it when
you're young. Not for yourself, young woman, peach your flub not
for yourself, softlorn.

Young women are for. Make that untrue, is their lookout.

Night-tinge leaked out of sky; now flat gray morn.

Could live quietly unflash, but listen, belles, just always tell
the unfair. It sacrifices you, but all hold hands and
won't, you need a job to feed your kid, you want a lover.
Live in case.

Snowflakes built rotating palaces on the way down. Crashcrust park-
ing lot crystalle.

RAIN COG

When I found in my starbuckle a new ire

I emerged from postlanguage

What'd I say?

Green clamp pulleywamp

Dallying open the silversound
That is the body's eon-noise and ecology

Divided mutter
In the supernal Vivian
How can I knock be clear about my intentions?

BLINK WHOLE HEAD IN IDENTIFICATORY TRANCE

When you don't see
  what I would have you see
 you sad me.
Open druthers, for I
j'adore your piggy light.

 Walking uphill in my fetish purse,
who my talking to?
Thunder in distance.
It's good to imagine audience.
 I hoped to write a VERY LONG
POEM, five pages typed,
 hung water bottle on belt loop,
off I went. Tall bluster
trees! I welcome you to the
land of cheesy me, openmouthed
 skullface cloud and lace cloud
pulled across it by storm wind.
Thunder

 ink of leather
heavy bloom
 growl in reverb valley
master, chew my head.

Here's the rain now   properly
lined up: stab gleam
THUNDER SONG

          Gonna stick you in the fire
          You'll be a bright gold baby

          Hey lightning hey hey thunder
          Gonna be a bright gold baby

          Blue wagon, lady flier
          Write a letter when you get there

          Hey noon and fire lady
          Make us a blue liquid snowball

          Make a planet built of lightning
          Learned how in lightning-basket-weaving class

At the community art center
I basket-wove a burning bush

Spoke to Moses—Here sir,
Whyncha let me talk to God

I kissed her outside lost my manners
I kissed her inside lost my face

But God she lost her whole fat body
She lost her great big coldframe

I asked for wysiwyg format
She said she couldn't do

I said I want to see what you look like
She said you soaked already do

I said I couldn't see nothing
She gave me paper "Draw me"
I drew and saw it, saw you too

Felt honey loll along the trench
I called it her I called it you

Why do I think I don't know?
I know just as well as I do

All to use artifice
Make life real for me and you

THE AUTONOMY OF ART HAS ITS ORIGINS IN THE CONCEALMENT OF LABOR

My heart beat very hard by itself.

A ROSE FOR GEORGE

If you don't have any control over your life and being happy
If you don't have any control over your life and be happy

A family in the wall
Mouse avenue in kitchen
A piece of cake
Looms oozing
Men and women are signs of life
Children are signs of life

When they put the cap on the oil well
I thought my life pollutes
Reading lamp = coal burn
My failures to love
To be friend family

When are we given the right to control
Fantasy?

Sixty-eight is a little bit of
Time in the world
To be more sentient
Kinder and "get up try again"
Body ow

I pretend if I were in New York
I could choose friends as I did in school
Fork into flesh of animal

Work all your life
Not hard enough! there are things undone

I was thinking you were my father
I wasn't here, then I was
Through you

Through an internal externalized
Spill

It bumps around the world
Tries not to be stupid

When Dad you grew up
Trying to intentionalize
Family back of you
George, young and into the continents
With problems

I already have what I desire
I just have it in the future
The structure of being is wanting
And like a fountain I suck up
Later
My excesses
A little evaporates
One day it's dry and drying
Means I'm done
Oh whatever you'll always be there no?

I can say when I die
"I was agent of clock"

They call it an alarm
I stopped having time to weed, friends

Started in dark
Light housed me

The TV is so loud I can't think
I'm sorry I can't be in that room

Nobody has yelled at me for a long time
Thank you

You exist because your dad and mom
And you tried to go away

Continuity sweepstakes
Freed under the cap

Get up orderly   loving

MAKE A MACHINE FOR MASTERING SELF

Grow your disposal
Chastity smell

In a room
Rectangle air
Allowed
Breathing there
Fantaseize

Lay down
Your cherry bright

You know how to make an asshole
With your fingers touching?
That's cherry-picking stance

The room is detachable pod
Walk it into disposal
Find the room in terror
In terror or terroir

Filter green
The color made by birds
Under time
They cull it from the aerie

Feel like
A terror maestra
See the cloud bear cherries
Oh my God
Let's get merried

SPELL

Ampersand to start the poem, keep you going, there's a
Next Anne Cunningham
Now intubated in white bed mountain range—
Event brought you here and event will blow you onward.

> this is the refrain from Anne harm
> refrain from all harm
> events blowing forward
> gentle your train
> refrain from all damn harm

Camp out in the mountains
Under fluorescent hiss and beep.
Nina (pet) put to sleep, ancient incontinent;
Now you mourn blood
Into your gastric tract.
Noble body, gather your
Guts, seal the passage:
Have to die sometime but curving intricate

Ampersand-tract says you'll
Meet us for breakfast.

this is the refrain from Anne harm
refrain from all harm
events blowing forward
gentle your train
refrain from all damn harm

ARRIVED DETACHING TOWARD THE UNION

If recombinatory guises suit you, prosody whore, make them
 do/be us.

TA

I put the diorama
  in a boat, color TV
showing the rerun

o'er and o'er
let it stink way down

and coral grew there.
  Covered it oar.

Let miserere deep.
Be mine for'air.

REGARDING THE USE-VALUE AND EXCHANGE VALUE OF ORGASMS, WITH A LIST OF ORGASM ANALOGUES

viz.:   Dead servant
           Smell garnet
           Drain goes down drain
I let him stay with me
Two years past patience
Because he could conjure
           Black silk dragged through blood brain barrier
           Black silk dragged through blood brain barrier
           Cog railway
           Axiom
Use value or exchange value?
He traded orgasms
I traded love-stance.
We lost our shirts.

Come, normative anomaly,
Repeatable difference, costly
And prized, normative wedge

In conscious norm, come
Oddity, trade you for memory.

Honey I love you for this fine minute
Honey your eyes have gone really buggy
I'm frightened, anticipant, oh hell, that's
Polaroid ripped back before it's developed
Sticky firework chemical
Gel burnt electrodes
Suffer the, suffer the, jailed
Axlotl, terminate its head,
I'm through with you

 : pleasure.

When the coagulant future returns,
Which is instant, even as happiness
Roams past the edges of nerve into room

The feeling's unsellable.
Never gets into poem.
I left my topography
Map on the picnic table
Rained and the tetons
Exposed their maché.

I see I'm aggressive, weirdly violent,
Cold-fingered
Won't mind being otherwise
Tell warm to me.
Goddamn these dactyls,
They crush labile rotica.
Kneejerk dactylic, see.
Needing to pee but I'm
Pushing this longer—

List of orgasm-metaphors
Commodity catalog
At outset of poem   Tried to turn
Time to material   Re-experienceable
Come back and see me some time.

If this poem is not desirable
But you've made yourself read it
You've been assigned it
You have a sane reason
Dear friend, that's a condom, you've
Inoculated your cock against insanity
(I'm figuring reader as male, why'd

I do that)—friend, there's a reason
(Really have to pee now)
To let pleasure be.

STATE

In the building where I work
I choose one of two diagonal paths

To one of a pair of identical stairwells
And mount to the same hallway

Cause I don't remember
State, state my home

Or I advance into a garden courtyard
Where no paths cross, no one meets there.

I was required to think of myself and for myself
By the State

Trained to think critically
By the State

To keep me from joining hands
With my neighbor.

I will now stop forever thinking for/of myself
And stop forever being free.

I mean this unironically.
I will have no thoughts

While blowing home a Government
made of poem.

The poem nation-projector
proposed a nation

off to the side.
I was assigned a body

and food, a room to work in
What did I make of it?

Have been sitting in this room hours
trying to make, and frustrated beyond

sense

return to the old project?

I gotta get out of here.

FLIES, POND

The nymphs half-god
transform.

Frogs' breath-circles
interrupting inverse tree.

Dark wavering instructs me
 moving picture of a tree.

Solid tree above, what do you
 look like when I am not me.

I have no vitreous eyeballs
 when I bloom dead.

 Voracious view,
climb tree from inside speedway,

willow, meet my will.

ANOTHER HUMAN MADE ME COME

That is fortunate. The interior muscles
 of the interior crawled around on themselves
  pulled [boogers] through body shield and I swear
left me open seize.
  I fear Haptic Treat
will be disappointed when he
 finds out I am dumb
 in my thought-heavens.
Not going to have to touch myself
memory swollen to fog lipid velvet
 postdimensional, where I contacted you
unprepare yourself. Tiny dried maple leaf
hits my shoulder. I rerouted wind
 inhaling. Wind dies
 next to me because it went away.
In other time I slept backwards
 swam quiet having my clit provoked
and fingers inside doing what
 what, I could not attend the ballet
 time befriends horned

fog to leave her workings agitant
 inside whorl room upon room.
Across my belly move
your lips and hair
 cause clear-blistering will
 to touch the phone, retouch
the phone, in the hammock in the yard
lightninged from satellite, not the
 message I want.

AIR ENVELOPE

The notebook margin
Lends to me
Its frugal axis, asking
Nothing, determinist
Of route, but blandly so.

"I didn't know."
I wrote it as if a poem
And my handy margin
Would profit me.

ROTTEN PLACE FOR CURRENCY TO GROW

Riding Branch

Sun and tree elaborate
A wild shadow-movie on notebook.
When I see you again, how slowly
Will you, in the, in me? Slow
Green severance.
Whether you care for me, I'd like to know.
If you irritate me, I still want you
To go in love with me.
Have not checked the news since left Ohio.
Am entire personal and wee.
In the woods I don't
Know Sudan highlands massacre
From tree.
Bloody hell. "A voice stains the canary birds."

A Gesture That Points Also Refracts

"I just invented Indo-European."
Texture: consisting of or related to text; the state of being
text. Cave-droppings. At the center, a stone-hole soup.
Pen logo says *OM* or *WO*.
"Here is the revisement."
"The unmoney is structured like a
Money is structured like a language."
Give that thought some currency.
Call your mother; call your banker; call your friend.
Across embedded networks swings
the thought, a baby clinging
to its underside, tight fists in hair.

"Nothing but this funnel! and what pours through it."

"You want more?"
"I could wish to partake of others' experience."
"—I assume you've heard of me?" ..in deep
startled voice

THE SUN-WENT-DOWN CALAMITY

means go in.

Coyotes! on far ridge.
Mosquitoes. Run.

If you add up scene,
    divide in half
to get the mean
you split apart the sun

 and see inside tree.
Writing so much about sun
it will get tired of me.
See you round.

I feel blind.
As bats, dark bullfrogs, crickets

outline valley.

I PRONOMIAL

deride and pony
consciousness
into halflit
stable.
One rides a horse
to go somewhere, of course.

The actual is
flickering a binary
between word and not-word.
I said I needed to have the end ofthe word for next.
But I did not needit. Next comes anyway
whatever you say.
I and time were made for/of each other.

A LANDSCAPE

I am away thinking
a false situation

making "work" out of mountains
when I am not working

the oracles are dumm
why are they so dumb

rainy day, ugly little room
I will make the mountains hurt

how will you do that how ill you
do so the oracles talk a lot

of shit like any
body make your own

sense
"mount harness"

CHICKEN

A poem goes to the other side. It's different there, but that's not why I wrote it. There's all there is, in the chicken joke. Where are you going with this.

DO FAIRLY PLEASANT THING

Sometimes I am permitted to return to a meadow
That is a place where logs were cut
That tenders a view—a mountain

I would not see for the trees.

Unscratched by thistles
I stroll a wood-chip road
Down meadow.

A rush of air past branches
Wind on skin
Unsimultaneous.

The road is to my eye

Unsightly and yet
It shares cause with the meadow
That is a place of forced permission.

THE UGLY NECK, *OR* MAKING BANK

Robins and cardinals blurt between furrows of storm.
A way energy has of being. It can caress itself.

I know you're in pain.
You're in pain.
If you're in no condition to consent,
it's rape.
If you're incapable of intoxication or unconsciousness
I still shouldn't rape you, system.

INFRA RES: COLOR ESSAYS

The light was out of my face
And defined the scene
Poured from my face
New hedges
Vomited
Possibilities
For hue
Were the only
One in the world
To be from/of my face.
The light had to be if my face.

Kinds of light:
green red yellow violet indigo blue orange clear UV hexed
white grainy thumping (Boise) gray (Ohio)
soggy (England) "normal" "here" no
other light?
I took a bath in spare liquid.
Lean down, color wall.
Will yellow, next to red, grab more
yellow waves, leaving red
more blue? It will.

I made clean lines ferment
By parking colors next to others.

The frame appears neutral
Need not be visual.

A neutral statement, halfway between
Right and left: "I would not

Reject a two-state solution
Outright."

"A [cold/warm] manner is a sign of [fear/power]."
"We can find a rational compromise but

"We'll get nowhere unless we maintain
Our weapons stockpile."

"I do wear makeup but don't like to
Look as if I did."

Red   flies toward eye

dark, but forward comes.

Hold death together with
eye shut.

Behind my eye
blue and green balloon-blurs
follow light
in the company of gammas and radio rays.

Whence this yellow page?
Aha! a sun trap, mid-notebook, slept agog.

The first
word on the yellow page is to be unctuous

BIRDPILE.

"BIRDPILE" in flight? or
grounded (dead)?

Meaning
brutally dragged in.

Dismounted sleep, stood in worry
lay down in worry
Remember more things to do
 Remember them
Wrote them down and say nay
I won't do that today
Today is for [green]

And we return to the question of the integration of color.

"Integration," heard aloud, contains within it
"gray." A sludgy neutral
fades.
Integration contains the word "shun."

I am going to go underground
and see what colors there are down there

Mines
  & Everyones.

I wake up and write continuously
With short pauses

Color, says Albers,
Is absolutely contextual.
So why do I like to
Be alone? What color are you
White woman?
Where context changes color to accord
That's the end of the war.
"Color changes according to context"
Color changes according to
Context and I act different when we are
With you.
For comfort in interpreting
Maximize contrast.
Day and night.
Day is the colored one.
Equally gone down (sun) for
You and for me. Later for you, westerner.

The sun-red hair
hides sun.
Blue probable
should I look up.

Infrares

The last time I was anywhere
I enjoyed erotica made only of color
 Fields placiding intramural
 Composting or illegal downshifting
 Of light and dark
  Colors derailing
Out of view, behind
 The station, acting intra.

Those colors were agents   From the Sun—

        (fluorescence—neon—stimulated gas—
                        diodes also—cased in plastic—
            also from the Sun)

If everything is from the Sun why praise it.

I didn't say I was praising.
 One who makes odes is an odor.
  Two who make odes are nearly perfume.

Some animal bothering the house, I won't look, it is from the Sun.

I split the sun into parts when I look (what praise for that?)

I don't split the sun into as many parts as rock shrimp do (27-part
 Color spectrum)

 But I can try to see colors I can't see, I don't think a rock shrimp can

 Try not to be angry not to be

A rock shrimp, I am angry about inequality and glad

 Too, fuck me
Whacked the fly but only a piece of it!
The rest flew away!

Parts of the spectrum are short, parts are long.
I wanted to locate unfairness
 In the color spectrum—
"It's all in how you see it"—
Oil distended the sea, rainbow worriers.
The dummkopf vision vice
Gets me stuck on things, bad habit

The peacock feather eerie deaf
　Holds light. That's glamor
　Where attention lingers static.

Immigration of light
Gray schtum
Feels a lot
Like parting/party.

　I was differentiating the page
From itself by writing.

　My headache's fisting
The sky is its border? (edge of atmosphere)
—The sun glances off multiparticles in
Atmosphere and I then can't see
　My stars. These are all wrong ways of saying
The poem for others to say
　　On screen.

ABOUT THE AUTHOR

The author of three previous full-length collections, Catherine Wagner was born in Burma during the Vietnam War to American military parents, and spent her early childhood in the Philippines, Indonesia, Yemen, and India before moving to the U.S. She received her MFA from the Iowa Writers' Workshop (where she studied with Jorie Graham and Donald Revell) and a PhD from the University of Utah. She has written criticism on Barbara Guest, Leslie Scalapino, and Harryette Mullen, among others, and has published chapbooks with the Dusie collective and other small presses. Her poems appear in the *Norton Anthology of Postmodern American Poetry* and *Out of Everywhere: Linguistically Innovative Poetry by Women in North America and the UK*, among other anthologies. She's currently an Associate Professor of English at Miami University in Ohio.

The state of the world calls out for poetry
to save it. LAWRENCE FERLINGHETTI

CITY LIGHTS SPOTLIGHT SHINES A LIGHT ON THE WEALTH
OF INNOVATIVE AMERICAN POETRY BEING WRITTEN TODAY.
WE PUBLISH ACCOMPLISHED FIGURES KNOWN IN THE
POETRY COMMUNITY AS WELL AS YOUNG EMERGING POETS,
USING THE CULTURAL VISIBILITY OF CITY LIGHTS TO BRING
THEIR WORK TO A WIDER AUDIENCE. IN DOING SO, WE ALSO
HOPE TO DRAW ATTENTION TO THOSE SMALL PRESSES
PUBLISHING SUCH AUTHORS. WITH CITY LIGHTS SPOTLIGHT,
WE WILL MAINTAIN OUR STANDARD OF INNOVATION AND
INCLUSIVENESS BY PUBLISHING HIGHLY ORIGINAL POETRY
FROM ACROSS THE CULTURAL SPECTRUM, REFLECTING
OUR LONGSTANDING COMMITMENT TO THIS MOST
ANCIENT AND STUBBORNLY ENDURING FORM OF ART.

CITY LIGHTS SPOTLIGHT

1

Norma Cole, *Where Shadows Will:*
Selected Poems 1988-2008

2

Anselm Berrigan, *Free Cell*

3

Andrew Joron, *Trance Archive:*
New and Selected Poems

4

Cedar Sigo, *Stranger in Town*

5

Will Alexander, *Compression & Purity*

6

Micah Ballard, *Waifs and Strays*

7

Julian Talamantez Brolaski, *Advice for Lovers*